The END...
WHAT HAPPENS NEXT?

ROBERT MORRIS

STUDY GUIDE

ISBN: 978-1-945529-88-7
eBook ISBN: 978-1-949399-79-0

We hope you hear from the Holy Spirit and receive God's richest blessings
from this book by Gateway Press. We want to provide the highest quality
resources that take the messages, music, and media of Gateway Church
to the world. For more information on other resources from Gateway
Publishing®, go to gatewaypublishing.com.

Gateway Press, an imprint of Gateway Publishing
700 Blessed Way
Southlake, Texas 76092
gatewaypublishing.com

Printed in the United States of America
19 20 21 22 23   5 4 3 2 1

CONTENTS

1

A TOUGH QUESTION

Many people have asked, "How could a loving God send people to hell?"
However, the real question is, "How could anyone reject a loving God?"

ENGAGE

If you had to eat the same meal every day for the rest of your life, what would you choose to eat?

WATCH

Watch "A Tough Question."
- Look for the evidence of the existence of God.
- Consider how God is both just and loving.

(If you are not able to watch this teaching on video, read the following. Otherwise, skip to the **Talk** section after viewing.)

READ

In this series, we will be talking about heaven, hell, and the Second Coming of Christ. First, we will deal with a tough question: *How could a loving God send anyone to hell?* Most people have either heard or wondered that exact question. The answer depends on two traits of God.

God Is a Just God.

There will never be an unjust judgment from God. This brings up another question that we need to answer first: *Would God send anyone to hell that had never heard the gospel?* What about a person who lived before Jesus or who lives in a place on this earth so remote that they never hear the gospel preached?

> For the wrath of God is revealed from heaven against all ungodliness and unrighteousness of men, who suppress the truth in unrighteousness, because what may be known of God is manifest in them, for God has shown *it* to them. For since the creation of the world His invisible *attributes* are clearly seen, being understood by the things that are made, *even* His eternal power and Godhead, so that they are without excuse (Romans 1:18-20).

Since the beginning of time, God has testified of Himself to every person so that no person has an excuse for an unrighteous life. Remember, God is a just God. You see, when we ask these questions, so many times we try to answer them with human logic. But we should never answer a biblical question without using the Bible. This passage makes it clear that God has testified to every person, both inwardly and externally. Every person has a conscience, which came from God. You cannot look up at the sky at night and fail to wonder, at some point in your life, if there is a God. God's creation testifies to itself, and God has revealed Himself to every person. Every person who seeks God will find Him. That is God's promise no matter where a person lives.

> I love those who love me,
> And those who seek me diligently will find me (Proverbs 8:17).

> And you will seek Me and find *Me*, when you search for Me with all your heart (Jeremiah 29:13).

> Ask, and it will be given to you; seek, and you will find; knock, and it will be opened to you. For everyone who asks receives, and he who seeks finds, and to him who knocks it will be opened. Or what man is there among you who, if his son asks for bread, will give him a stone? Or if he asks for a fish, will he give him a serpent? If you then, being evil, know how to give good gifts to your children, how much more will your Father who is in heaven give good things to those who ask Him! (Matthew 7:7-11).

> And He has made from one blood every nation of men to dwell on all the face of the earth, and has determined their preappointed

times and the boundaries of their dwellings, so that they should seek the Lord, in the hope that they might grope for Him and find Him, though He is not far from each one of us; for in Him we live and move and have our being, as also some of your own poets have said, "For we are also His offspring" (Acts 17:26-28).

God is a just God. He is talking to the whole world. We all go back to Adam. If a person will make an effort, God will reveal Himself to him. *No person will ever receive an unjust judgment from God.*

God Is a Loving God.

So how can a loving God send a person to hell? We need to answer this question from a biblical perspective and from God's perspective. God did not create hell for people. God sent His Son so that no one would ever have to go to hell, whether or not they knew about Jesus, before or after He came.

The Lord is not slack concerning *His* promise, as some count slackness, but is longsuffering toward us, not willing that any should perish but that all should come to repentance (2 Peter 3:9).

To answer this question, we will look at this from a different perspective—the perspective of the inexcusable, rebellious rejection of a loving God. Four stories in the Bible demonstrate this.

Isaiah 14 and Revelation 12 tell of the inexcusable rebellion of Lucifer and a third of heaven. Lucifer was the worship leader in heaven. He was so beautiful and so persuasive that he convinced a third of the angels to rebel. These beings did not have a bad Father, they were never mistreated, and God never did anything to warrant their rejection. Still, they rejected Him and rebelled. Satan was hurled to the earth like lightning. (I personally believe that was when hell was created.) Matthew 25:41 tells us that hell was prepared for the devil and his angels.

Have you ever been rejected? Did it hurt? It's the greatest hurt we experience. God was hurt when He was rejected. We are made in His image, which is why we hurt too when we experience rejection.

The angels rejected God, and then He created man in His own image: with a free will. In Genesis 3 Adam and Eve also reject God—a God they know and walk with every day. There was no sin, and it was a perfect environment in the Garden of Eden. They had a perfect marriage, perfect health, perfect bodies—everything was perfect. Yet Adam and Eve rejected God.

The third story is Jesus. We'll come back to it, but Jesus came to this earth and was so rejected that they killed Him.

The fourth story is in Revelation 20. Jesus rules on the earth while Satan is bound for a thousand years. When he is released, Satan then leads people in rebellion against God.

God has been longsuffering throughout history. The prophets were broken-hearted men begging people to return to God. All God wanted was a family, and that is what He gets at the end of time. It's all He gets. The heavens and the earth as we know them are destroyed. The only thing left are the people who *chose* to be His family. God created us with a free will, which is the greatest thing He gave mankind in creation. He gave us a choice.

We don't celebrate when a vacuum cleaner cleans a room, but if your kids clean their rooms, you celebrate. When someone with a free will loves you, it's meaningful. It blesses God and makes Him happy when you worship because you have a choice. He thinks it is wonderful; that's why God inhabits the praises of His people.

Would God send someone to hell? No, He wouldn't, but people send themselves to hell all the time. You have a choice—you need to understand that. Your eternal destination is chosen by you, not God. People want to blame God, but it's your choice where you spend eternity. Nobody's going to force you to accept Jesus Christ, to go to church, or read the Bible. You will do it because you voluntarily choose to love God.

It is true that God chose us before we chose Him, but God chose *everyone in the world*—not just believers. The only people in heaven are those who chose Him back.

Isaiah talks about Jesus:

Now let me sing to my Well-beloved
A song of my Beloved regarding His vineyard:
My Well-beloved has a vineyard
On a very fruitful hill.
He dug it up and cleared out its stones,
And planted it with the choicest vine.

He built a tower in its midst,
And also made a winepress in it;
So He expected *it* to bring forth *good* grapes,
But it brought forth wild grapes.
"And now, O inhabitants of Jerusalem and men of Judah,
Judge, please, between Me and My vineyard.
What more could have been done to My vineyard
That I have not done in it?
Why then, when I expected *it* to bring forth *good* grapes,
Did it bring forth wild grapes? (Isaiah 5:1-4).

The tower refers to the pulpit or the Church, and the winepress refers to the Holy Spirit.

Woe to those who rise early in the morning,
That they may follow intoxicating drink;
Who continue until night, *till* wine inflames them!
The harp and the strings,
The tambourine and flute,
And wine are in their feasts;
But they do not regard the work of the Lord,
Nor consider the operation of His hands.
Therefore my people have gone into captivity,
Because *they have* no knowledge;
Their honorable men *are* famished,
And their multitude dried up with thirst.
Therefore Sheol has enlarged itself

And opened its mouth beyond measure;
Their glory and their multitude and their pomp,
And he who is jubilant, shall descend into it.
People shall be brought down,
Each man shall be humbled,
And the eyes of the lofty shall be humbled (Isaiah 5:11–15).

Look at verse 14: Sheol—Hell—has enlarged itself. Hell was not created for people. God says He created this vineyard, but because man rejected Him, hell was enlarged. Jesus talks more about hell than heaven because He doesn't want people to go to hell. But because people rejected and resisted Him, hell was enlarged.

This is the third story, which I said we'd come back to. Watch what Jesus says about the vineyard, the tower, and the winepress:

Hear another parable: There was a certain landowner who planted a vineyard and set a hedge around it, dug a winepress in it and built a tower. And he leased it to vinedressers and went into a far country. Now when vintage-time drew near, he sent his servants to the vinedressers, that they might receive its fruit. And the vinedressers took his servants, beat one, killed one, and stoned another. Again he sent other servants, more than the first, and they did likewise to them. Then last of all he sent his son to them, saying, "They will respect my son." But when the vinedressers saw the son, they said among themselves, "This is the heir. Come, let us kill him and seize his inheritance." So they took him and cast *him* out of the vineyard and killed *him* (Matthew 21:33–39).

They took the Son and killed Him. This is the third story: the inexcusable, rebellious rejection of Jesus Christ.

So the tough question is not, "How can God send someone to hell?" The tough question that I can't answer is "How can anyone reject a loving God?" It's your choice.

NOTES

_____

_____

_____

_____

_____

_____

_____

_____

_____

_____

_____

_____

TALK

These questions can be used for group discussion or personal reflection:

Question 1

When did you first hear or learn about hell? What did you believe about it then?

_____

_____

_____

_____

Question 2

What do you think people are really wrestling with when they ask, "How could a loving God send anyone to hell?"

_____

_____

_____

_____

Question 3
Why is rejecting God "inexcusable" and "rebellious"?

_____

_____

_____

_____

Question 4
Read Romans 1:18-20. What "normal" experiences in your own
life (such as seeing the stars on a cloudless night) have led you to
worship God?

_____

_____

_____

_____

Question 5

Read 2 Peter 3:9. Hell was not made for people, and God sent His Son so that no one would ever have to go there. How do you think God feels when people have to pay eternal consequences for rejecting Him?

_____

_____

_____

_____

PRAY

If studying alone, ask the Holy Spirit to reveal the truth about Himself to you. If in a group, take some time to pray for each other as you think about the truths discussed in this session.

EXPLORE

Do you want to go deeper with this teaching? Here are some additional things to think about, pray for, or write about in your journal throughout the next week.

Key Quote

Would God send someone to hell? No, He wouldn't, but people send themselves to hell all the time. Your eternal destination is chosen by you, not God.

Why did God give us a free will? What does this say about His character?

_____

_____

_____

_____

Key Verses
Romans 1:18-20; Isaiah 5:1-15; Matthew 21:33-39
What truths stand out to you as you read these verses?

_____

_____

What is the Holy Spirit saying to you through these Scriptures?

_____

_____

Key Question
Why *would* someone reject a loving God and choose to be separated from Him?

Key Prayer

Heavenly Father, we thank You for Your immeasurable goodness. Thank You for speaking to us through the beauty of Your creation as well as in our hearts. We repent of any area where we have resisted or rejected You. Thank You for giving us everything we need for life, both now and for eternity. In Jesus' name, Amen.

2

SOME EASY QUESTIONS

The answers to many common questions about heaven can be found in the Bible.

RECAP

In the previous session, we learned that God is a just and loving God who does not want anyone to go to hell. People choose their eternal destination based on their own free will.

Did you have a chance to share God's love with anyone new this past week?

ENGAGE

What was the worst pet you ever owned?

WATCH

Watch "Some Easy Questions."

- Look for some of the common misconceptions about heaven.
- Consider how your thinking about heaven (and hell) affects your perspective and your actions.

(If you are not able to watch this teaching on video, read the following. Otherwise, skip to the **Talk** section after viewing.)

READ

We are going to answer ten easy questions about heaven.

> When He opened the fifth seal, I saw under the altar the souls of those who had been slain for the word of God and for the testimony which they held. And they cried with a loud voice, saying, "How long, O Lord, holy and true, until You judge and avenge our blood on those who dwell on the earth?" Then a white robe was given to each of them; and it was said to them that they should rest a little while longer, until both *the number of* their fellow servants and their brethren, who would be killed as they *were,* was completed (Revelation 6:9–11).

1. Will We Have Bodies in Heaven?

Some people think we'll be like air or a wisp of smoke in heaven. But why then do the martyrs get robes? First Corinthians 15:47–49 says,

> The first man *was* of the earth, *made* of dust; the second Man *is* the Lord from heaven. As *was* the *man* of dust, so also *are* those *who are made* of dust; and as *is* the heavenly *Man,* so also *are* those *who are* heavenly. And as we have borne the image of the *man* of dust, we shall also bear the image of the heavenly *Man.*

In other words, Jesus is our example. He had an earthly body that suffered and died, but after the Resurrection He had a heavenly, glorified body. The body walked on the earth, ate food, and walked through walls. Our bodies and spirits reunite at the second coming. Jesus said, "Touch me." There is a coming together of the terrestrial and celestial body, which you can read about in depth in 1 Corinthians 15. When we bury people, we bury them with their feet to the East and their heads to the West; "For as the lightning comes from the east and flashes to the west, so also will the coming of the Son of Man be" (Matthew 24:27). We bury with the end in mind, so that they come out of the grave facing Jesus.

2. Will We Go to Heaven Immediately?

The Bible teaches that when we die, we immediately go to heaven. The martyrs in Revelation 6 were in heaven after their death *before* the second coming. Jesus told the thief on the cross that he would be with Him "today" in paradise. Second Corinthians 5:8 says, "We are confident, yes, well pleased rather to be absent from the body and to be present with the Lord."

3. Will We Be Able to Communicate?

Yes. The martyrs had the ability to communicate in heaven. They cried out in loud voices.

4. Will We Have Emotions?

The martyrs cared deeply about what was happening on earth. Emotions are part of our soul, of our personhood. We will still have emotions, just like God, who is *not* a sterile, emotionless being.

Heaven rejoices when a sinner repents. There will be unimaginable and incomparable joy and peace in heaven.

5. Will We Know Everything?

No, we won't. The martyrs asked God a question. Jesus said that no one except the Father knows the date of Jesus' return. The idea that we will know everything comes from confusing two Scriptures.

> For now we see in a mirror, dimly, but then face to face. Now I know in part, but then I shall know just as I also am known (1 Corinthians 13:12).

> Beloved, now we are children of God; and it has not yet been revealed what we shall be, but we know that when He is revealed, we shall be like Him, for we shall see Him as He is (1 John 3:2).

The verse from 1 Corinthians just says that we will know others and they will know us. The verse from 1 John means that we will have a new, heavenly perspective. We will be like God in the same way Adam and Eve were like God, in that we were created in His image. We will not be omniscient.

6. Will We Know What's Happening on Earth?

The martyrs knew what was happening on earth when they asked about avenging their blood. Hebrews 12:1 says the dead saints are "witnessing" what was going on right then, and Luke 15:7 says people in heaven were rejoicing over one sinner who repented on earth. This all happens before the return of Christ. No person will repent after the return of Christ.

7. Will We Remember Our Lives on Earth?

The martyrs remembered that they were murdered. We will remember our lives on earth because it will make us grateful. Our memories of earth will help us appreciate heaven. However, memories of earth will torment those in hell.

8. Will We Know People?

First Corinthians 13 says we will know people as we are known. In fact, we will finally understand people. There may be some people there we didn't expect to see—or who didn't expect to see us. In Matthew 8:11, Jesus says, "And I say to you that many will come from east and west, and sit down with Abraham, Isaac, and Jacob in the kingdom of heaven." We're going to sit down with Abraham and Moses and ask them what was going on in their minds! Or ask Peter why he was always blurting out something.

9. Will It Be Boring?

Some people think that hell is going to be the fun, exciting place. Satan has planted the idea in us that heaven is going to be a boring church service, and we'll just be floating around on clouds playing harps, while hell is a big party. But if you don't know about heaven, you won't be motivated to choose it or recommend it to others. In fact, we will be reunited with family and friends. We'll be in glorified bodies able to travel across the universe at the speed of thought. Eat all you want and never gain a pound! Heaven will be the most wonderful place imaginable.

Don Piper, in his book *90 Minutes in Heaven*, describes his experience in heaven when he was clinically dead for 90 minutes.[1] It was like an incredible family reunion, and he had never felt so fully alive and joyful. Here is a description from Revelation:

> Now I saw a new heaven and a new earth, for the first heaven and the first earth had passed away. Also there was no more sea. Then I, John, saw the holy city, New Jerusalem, coming down out of heaven from God, prepared as a bride adorned for her husband. And I heard a loud voice from heaven saying, "Behold, the tabernacle of God *is* with men, and He will dwell with them, and they shall be His people. God Himself will be with them *and be* their God. And God will wipe away every tear from their eyes; there shall be no more death, nor sorrow, nor crying. There shall be no more pain, for the former things have passed away."
>
> Then He who sat on the throne said, "Behold, I make all things new." And He said to me, "Write, for these words are true and faithful" (Revelation 21:1–5).

The greatest thing about heaven will be the fellowship we will have with fellow believers and with the Father. The worst thing about hell is that you will never see or talk with anyone.

1. Don Piper, *90 Minutes in Heaven* (Baker Publishing: Grand Rapids, 2004).

10. Who Will Be There?

This is the most important question. Scripture answers this.

And He said to me, "It is done! I am the Alpha and the Omega, the Beginning and the End. I will give of the fountain of the water of life freely to him who thirsts (Revelation 21:6).

And the Spirit and the bride say, "Come!" And let him who hears say, "Come!" And let him who thirsts come. Whoever desires, let him take the water of life freely (Revelation 22:17).

If you confess with your mouth the Lord Jesus and believe in your heart that God has raised Him from the dead, you will be saved (Romans 10:9).

For "whoever calls on the name of the Lord shall be saved" (Romans 10:13).

Who will be there? Those who believe in the Lord Jesus Christ and call on His name.

NOTES

_____

_____

_____

TALK

These questions can be used for group discussion or personal reflection:

Question 1
What questions have you had about heaven?

_____

_____

_____

_____

Question 2
Why do you think it's so hard to imagine what heaven will be like?

_____

_____

_____

_____

Question 3

Read Matthew 8:11. Which believer, from any time in history, would you most like to sit and talk with in heaven?

_____

_____

_____

_____

Question 4

Of the 10 common questions about heaven, which stood out to you the most? Why?

_____

_____

_____

_____

Question 5

Have you ever worried that heaven will be boring? Why do you think many people think that way?

_____

_____

_____

_____

PRAY

If studying alone, ask the Holy Spirit to reveal the truth about Himself to you. If in a group, take some time to pray for each other as you think about the truths discussed in this session.

EXPLORE

Do you want to go deeper with this teaching? Here are some additional things to think about, pray for, or write about in your journal throughout the next week.

Key Quote

Who will be there? Those who believe in the Lord, Jesus Christ, and call on His name.

Who do you expect to be in heaven with you? What are you looking forward to most about heaven?

_____

_____

_____

_____

Key Verses
Revelation 21:1–6, 22:7; 2 Corinthians 5:8; Romans 10:9
What truths stand out to you as you read these verses?

_____

_____

What is the Holy Spirit saying to you through these Scriptures?

_____

_____

Key Question
In what ways does thinking about your future life in heaven affect your perspective about life on earth?

Key Prayer
Father, thank You for all the amazing things You have prepared for us in heaven. Thank You for making heaven available to us by Your grace, at no cost to us. Speak to those in our lives who need to know Jesus and help us lead them to Him. In Jesus' name, Amen.

3

A TOUGH MESSAGE

The Bible refers to hell 167 times and describes it as a real place of eternal torment.

RECAP

In the previous section, we learned about what it will be like in heaven and who will be there with us. It will be a beautiful place that we will enjoy forever.

Did you find yourself thinking about heaven more than usual this past week?

ENGAGE

What is the worst place you ever visited? Why was it so bad?

WATCH

Watch "A Tough Message."

- Notice the many different opinions about hell.
- Watch how Jesus addresses hell and why He so strongly warns against going there.

(If you are not able to watch this teaching on video, read the following. Otherwise, skip to the **Talk** section after viewing.)

READ

Jesus considered the topic of hell important enough to teach about it 33 times. He talked more about hell than he did heaven. Why did He do that? Because He was filled with compassion to keep people from going to this terrible place.

The Bible talks about hell 167 times, yet many pastors, theologians, and even denominations are distancing themselves from hell or denying the existence of it today. According to one survey, seventy-one percent of seminary students in the United States do not believe in a literal hell or heaven.

Here's the problem: If you don't believe in hell, you can't believe in heaven, because Jesus and the Bible teach about both. In my opinion, to deny hell is to deny Jesus and the Bible.

There are four groups who do not believe in hell:

- **Atheists** do not believe in hell because they do not believe in God. They believe we evolved from nothing, and once we die, we cease to exist.
- **Annihilationists** believe that the saved go to heaven and the unsaved are annihilated (cease to exist).
- **Ultimate reconciliationists** believe that those who go to hell are punished and purified by God. Eventually everyone, including fallen angels and Satan, are reconciled to God, and hell becomes empty.
- **Universalists** believe that every person goes to heaven, regardless of their religious lifestyle or moral choices. Hitler,

Stalin, and terrorists will be in heaven whether they like it
or not.

In Luke 16, Jesus tells us about hell. This is a *true story*, not a
parable or a simile. Jesus says there is a certain, specific rich person
and a beggar with a name.

> There was a certain rich man who was clothed in purple and fine
> linen and fared sumptuously every day. But there was a certain
> beggar named Lazarus, full of sores, who was laid at his gate,
> desiring to be fed with the crumbs which fell from the rich man's
> table. Moreover the dogs came and licked his sores. So it was
> that the beggar died, and was carried by the angels to Abraham's
> bosom. The rich man also died and was buried. And being in
> torments in Hades, he lifted up his eyes and saw Abraham afar off,
> and Lazarus in his bosom.
>
> Then he cried and said, "Father Abraham, have mercy on me,
> and send Lazarus that he may dip the tip of his finger in water and
> cool my tongue; for I am tormented in this flame." But Abraham
> said, "Son, remember that in your lifetime you received your good
> things, and likewise Lazarus evil things; but now he is comforted
> and you are tormented. And besides all this, between us and you
> there is a great gulf fixed, so that those who want to pass from here
> to you cannot, nor can those from there pass to us."
>
> Then he said, "I beg you therefore, father, that you would
> send him to my father's house, for I have five brothers, that he
> may testify to them, lest they also come to this place of torment."
> Abraham said to him, "They have Moses and the prophets; let them

hear them." And he said, "No, father Abraham; but if one goes to them from the dead, they will repent." But he said to him, "If they do not hear Moses and the prophets, neither will they be persuaded though one rise from the dead" (Luke 16:19–31).

Notice the word *torment*. The word is used in four different ways in this passage. Notice the word *flame* as well. Jesus describes hell as a place of torment and flame. This ends all debate about hell, because Jesus refers to a specific man who is in hell. It is a place of fire. The New Testament refers to hell as a place of fire 32 times: lake of, everlasting, eternal, unquenchable fire. Jesus Himself refers to hell as fire 19 times.

It also ends debate about whether hell is a place of torment. Verses 23, 24, 25, and 28 all describe hell as a place of torment. *Torment* in the Greek means "acute pain from a debilitating disease," a "rack of torture," or an "intense fire hot enough to melt gold."

So what happens when a person goes to hell?

He Desires Comfort

The rich man asked for just the tip of Lazarus' finger—not a bucket or glass—to be dipped in water to cool his tongue. Remember, hell was not created for man. It was prepared for Satan and his followers and enlarged by necessity, not by design:

Then He will also say to those on the left hand, "Depart from Me, you cursed, into the everlasting fire prepared for the devil and his angels" (Matthew 25:41).

Jesus did not prepare hell for you, but He did prepare heaven for you. In John 14:2, He says, "I go to prepare a place for you."

He Expresses Concern

The rich man immediately asks to send Lazarus to his brothers, to warn his family. How many of our family or coworkers will wonder why we didn't tell them about this place? Your family and friends will spend eternity in hell if you don't help them!

He Seeks Consolation

The man tried to convince himself that if someone would rise from the dead, *maybe* his family would believe. But he was told that if they wouldn't hear the Bible (Moses and the prophets), then they won't be persuaded even if one would rise from the grave. This is a direct reference to Jesus rising from the dead.

This story describes hell before the resurrection of Christ. All who died before His resurrection went to a place of waiting. There was a place of hell, where people were tormented, and there was Abraham's bosom, a place of waiting for Old Testament saints. The Bible says that when Jesus died, before He ascended, He descended into the lower parts and led the Old Testament saints to paradise. He even said to the thief on the cross, "Today you will be with me in paradise."

There is also a future hell after the Second Coming. The Bible tells us some things about future hell that we need to understand. There are two physical properties on earth that keep us mentally stable: light and solid. Light helps us gain our bearings. There is no light in hell; Matthew 8:12 describes hell as a place of utter darkness (blackness). No matter how hard you try to adjust your eyes in hell, you will never be able to see. You will not be able to see another person. (The rich man saw Abraham because this was before the resurrection of Christ.)

The second physical property is solid. Being able to touch or hold something keeps us mentally stable on this earth. Revelation chapters 9, 11, 17, and 20 describe hell as a bottomless pit. You can never touch anything no matter how you try to reach. You are suspended away from everything and every person, while in total darkness.

There are also two emotional properties that keep us stable in this life: rest and hope. When we go through something difficult, we look forward to rest—a break from the pain and torment. Revelation 14:11 says, "And the smoke of their torment ascends forever and ever; and they have no rest day or night."

There is also no hope. On this earth, we always have hope that it can get better. You can always turn to God. But in hell, there is no hope. Every person in hell will have some thought such as, "When I have been here 10,000 centuries, I will not have one less second of time to spend here."

Jesus used the word *Gehenna* to describe hell. The Jewish people understood this word. Gehenna means the Valley of Henna, which is a valley south of the city of Jerusalem. In that valley, there was always a fire where they burned the refuse of the city. They also burned the bodies of paupers and executed criminals there. You could smell flesh burning.

The Canaanites and idolatrous Israelites sacrificed their children to the god Molech in a fire that burned continuously. They actually made their children march into the fire alive. Jesus used a phrase every Jewish person understood about Gehenna: "Where there was weeping, wailing, and gnashing of teeth." It described the fear and pain of these children as they were burned alive. This is how Jesus described hell. He was trying to make sure that people understood how bad it was, so that we don't go there.

If your neighbor doesn't know the Lord, he will go to a place of torment for all eternity. It is your responsibility, before it is too late, to tell your neighbor that by calling on the name of the Lord, he can be saved.

NOTES

_____

_____

_____

_____

_____

_____

_____

_____

TALK

These questions can be used for group discussion or personal reflection:

Question 1

Read Luke 16:19–31. What do you think Jesus wanted to communicate to us through this story?

_____

_____

_____

_____

Question 2

Read Mark 9:43–48 and Matthew 13:41–42. How do these passages describe hell?

_____

_____

_____

_____

Question 3
What are the physical and emotional properties on earth that keep us mentally stable? How will hell be different from earth?

_____

_____

_____

_____

Question 4
Why did Jesus use the word *Gehenna* to describe hell?

_____

_____

_____

_____

PRAY

If studying alone, ask the Holy Spirit to reveal the truth about Himself to you. If in a group, take some time to pray for each other as you think about the truths discussed in this session.

EXPLORE

Do you want to go deeper with this teaching? Here are some additional things to think about, pray for, or write about in your journal throughout the next week.

Key Quote

> *Every person in hell will have some thought such as, "When I have been here 10,000 centuries, I will not have one less second of time to spend here."*

Why do you think people want to deny the existence of hell?

_____

_____

_____

_____

Key Verses

Luke 16:19–31; Matthew 25:41; Revelation 14:11

What truths stand out to you as you read these verses?

_____

_____

What is the Holy Spirit saying to you through these Scriptures?

_____

_____

Key Question

Whom do you need to share the gospel with this week?

Key Prayer

Father, thank You for making a way for us to choose eternal life through Jesus Christ. Help us to share the gospel with the people in our sphere of influence so they can be spared from eternal torment. Holy Spirit, please give us boldness as we share our faith. In Jesus' name, Amen.

4

A TOUGH DAY

We are saved by grace through faith alone, but how we live on earth matters. Believers and unbelievers will be judged according to their works.

RECAP

In the previous session, we learned that hell is a real place of eternal torment. It is our responsibility to share the gospel with others now while there is still time.

Did you have any new opportunities to share the gospel with others this past week?

ENGAGE

What is your favorite thing about back-to-school season?

WATCH

Watch "A Tough Day."

- Look for who will be subject to judgment.
- Watch for when and how judgment will come to believers and unbelievers.

(If you are not able to watch this teaching on video, read the following. Otherwise, skip to the **Talk** section after viewing.)

READl

I s there a judgment day coming? Absolutely. Will everyone be judged? Yes. Will both believers and unbelievers be judged? Yes. We will be judged according to grace *and* according to our works on the appropriate day. Here are some Scriptures about judgment.

The Lord knows how to deliver the godly out of temptations and to reserve the unjust under punishment for the day of judgment (2 Peter 2:9).

But the heavens and the earth *which* are now preserved by the same word, are reserved for fire until the day of judgment and perdition of ungodly men (2 Peter 3:7).

But I say to you that for every idle word men may speak, they will give account of it in the day of judgment (Matthew 12:36).

It is appointed for men to die once, but after this the judgment (Hebrews 9:27).

For God will bring every work into judgment,
Including every secret thing,
Whether good or evil (Ecclesiastes 12:14).

The sea gave up the dead who were in it, and Death and Hades delivered up the dead who were in them. And they were judged, each one according to his works (Revelation 20:13).

And if you call on the Father, who without partiality judges according to each one's work, conduct yourselves throughout the time of your stay *here* in fear (1 Peter 1:17).

For the Son of Man will come in the glory of His Father with His angels, and then He will reward each according to his works (Matthew 16:27).

And behold, I am coming quickly, and My reward *is* with Me, to give to every one according to his work (Revelation 22:12).

Each and every—this includes all of us. These verses show that we will all—including believers—be *judged* and *rewarded*, according to our works. But we are saved only by grace:

For by grace you have been saved through faith, and that not of yourselves; *it is* the gift of God, not of works, lest anyone should boast (Ephesians 2:8–9).

How do we explain that we are saved by grace but judged by our works? We have to distinguish between our belief and our behavior. Our **belief** determines *where* we spend eternity. Our **behavior** determines *how* we spend eternity. In heaven, people are going to be rewarded for their works, and in hell, people will be punished for their works.

There are two judgments: The judgment seat of Christ and the Great White Throne Judgment. At the judgment seat of Christ, every person there is a believer. At the Great White Throne judgment, every person there is an unbeliever. These judgments are *not* for the purpose of determining your belief. Your belief has already determined which judgment you will attend. At each judgment, your behavior will be judged. It matters how you live and what you do on this earth. Scripture says that your belief will alter your behavior. Faith will give you the desire and the power to serve God.

Grace and works are married in Scripture, and it is easy to understand these concepts when you separate belief and behavior.

The Judgment Seat of Christ

These Scriptures are written to believers:

For we must all appear before the judgment seat of Christ, that each one may receive the things *done* in the body, according to what he has done, whether good or bad (2 Corinthians 5:10).

But why do you judge your brother? Or why do you show contempt for your brother? For we shall all stand before the judgment seat of Christ (Romans 14:10).

First Corinthians is the second letter Paul wrote to the Corinthian church. He mentions an earlier letter and straightens out some issues with them. One of their points of contention is who led them to Christ. Paul says they need to understand that Jesus is the judge, and we will stand before Him, not before Paul or Apollos.

Who then is Paul, and who *is* Apollos, but ministers through whom you believed, as the Lord gave to each one? I planted, Apollos watered, but God gave the increase. So then neither he who plants is anything, nor he who waters, but God who gives the increase. Now he who plants and he who waters are one, and **each** one will receive his own reward according to his own labor.

For we are God's fellow workers; you are God's field, *you are* God's building. According to the grace of God which was given to me, as a wise master builder I have laid the foundation, and another builds on it. But let **each** one take heed how he builds on it. For no other foundation can anyone lay than that which is laid, which is Jesus Christ. Now if anyone builds on this foundation *with* gold, silver, precious stones, wood, hay, straw, **each** one's work will become clear; for the **Day** will declare it, because it will be revealed by fire; and the fire will test **each** one's work, of what sort it is. If anyone's work which he has built on *it* endures, he will receive a reward. If anyone's work is burned, he will suffer loss; but he himself will be saved, yet so as through fire (1 Corinthians 3:5–15, emphasis added).

You can be a believer and build on the foundation of Jesus Christ with wood, hay, and straw *or* with gold, silver, and precious stones. Your works will be tested, and eternal works will be rewarded. Jesus talks about this in Matthew:

> Take heed that you do not do your charitable deeds before men, to be seen by them. Otherwise you have no reward from your Father in heaven. Therefore, when you do a charitable deed, do not sound a trumpet before you as the hypocrites do in the synagogues and in the streets, that they may have glory from men. Assuredly, I say to you, they have their reward. But when you do a charitable deed, do not let your left hand know what your right hand is doing, that your charitable deed may be in secret; and your Father who sees in secret will Himself reward you openly (Matthew 6:1-4).

Notice that you can do something good and lose your reward for it because of the way you do it. Notice the word *Himself*. The Father is going to reward you *personally*. He won't just give a big "Y'all done good" to a group of a billion people. You will meet the Father personally, and He will reward you personally.

First John 2:28 says, "And now, little children, abide in Him, that when He appears, we may have confidence and not be ashamed before Him at His coming." Clearly your behavior matters if you could be ashamed when Jesus comes. You will be ashamed if you didn't serve Him, love Him, or walk with Him.

Heaven will consist of cities. In Luke 19, Jesus talks about giving faithful stewards cities to rule over. Jesus told *believers* to store up treasures for *yourselves* in heaven. You will need resources to do business in heaven. Heaven is not going to be just floating on clouds. It will be a perfect heaven and earth with no sin, but we will be living our lives. We will have responsibilities based upon how we handled responsibility here on earth. Someone will get to be the mayor of those cities. How many believers will get to heaven and not have many rewards or responsibilities?

The Great White Throne Judgment

Then I saw a great white throne and Him who sat on it, from whose face the earth and the heaven fled away. And there was found no place for them. And I saw the dead, small and great, standing before God, and books were opened. And another book was opened, which is the Book of Life. And the dead were judged according to their works, by the things which were written in the books. The sea gave up the dead who were in it, and Death and Hades delivered up the dead who were in them. And they were judged, each one according to his works (Revelation 20:11-13).

You are in the Book of Life if you are a believer, but there are books that contain the deeds we have done. Unbelievers will receive different degrees of punishment. Hitler will be punished more than a person of good character and action who just fails to accept Jesus.

Woe to you, Chorazin! Woe to you, Bethsaida! For if the mighty works which were done in you had been done in Tyre and Sidon, they would have repented long ago in sackcloth and ashes. But I

> say to you, it will be more tolerable for Tyre and Sidon in the day
> of judgment than for you. And you, Capernaum, who are exalted
> to heaven, will be brought down to Hades; for if the mighty works
> which were done in you had been done in Sodom, it would have
> remained until this day. But I say to you that it shall be more
> tolerable for the land of Sodom in the day of judgment than for you.
> (Matthew 11:21-24).

More tolerable means "easier or less suffering." Jesus said that if the same works He did in Chorazin and Bethsaida that had been done in Tyre and Sidon, they would have repented. Sodom would have repented if its people had seen the works done in Capernaum.

Believers are storing up rewards in heaven, and unbelievers are storing up judgment in hell. In the first chapter of Romans, Paul talks about how people rejected Jesus. This topic carries over into Romans 2.

> But in accordance with your hardness and your impenitent heart
> you are treasuring up for yourself wrath in the day of wrath and
> revelation of the righteous judgment of God (Romans 2:5).

Nonbelievers, according to the same degrees as your hardness— because of how you are acting—you are treasuring up for yourself *wrath* in hell.

There are degrees of judgment. James 3:1 even says that believers who are teachers will receive a stricter judgment.

When I was young, I hung out at the skating rink. I had started smoking and getting into trouble. My father dropped me off, but unknown to me, he waited around and watched me. When he picked me up later, he punished me for each cigarette I had smoked. I thought, "If I had known, I would have acted differently."

The Father is watching. You will be rewarded according to your works if you are a believer, and you will be punished according to your works if you are an unbeliever. *You* get to choose which of the two judgment seats you stand before—but you only have that choice while you are still alive on this earth. "It is appointed for men to die once, but after this the judgment" (Hebrews 9:27).

NOTES

_____

_____

_____

_____

_____

_____

_____

_____

_____

TALK

These questions can be used for group discussion or personal reflection:

Question 1

What is the main difference between the judgment seat of Christ and the Great White Throne judgment?

_____

_____

_____

_____

Question 2

Read 1 Corinthians 3:9–15. How will believers' works be judged?

_____

_____

_____

_____

Question 3
According to Matthew 6:1-4, how can believers lose their reward for good works?

_____

_____

_____

_____

Question 4
Read Matthew 11:21-24. Why did Jesus say the punishment would be worse for Chorazin and Bethsaida than the other cities?

_____

_____

_____

_____

PRAY

If studying alone, ask the Holy Spirit to reveal the truth about Himself to you. If in a group, take some time to pray for each other as you think about the truths discussed in this session.

EXPLORE

Do you want to go deeper with this teaching? Here are some additional things to think about, pray for, or write about in your journal throughout the next week.

Key Quote

We have to distinguish between our belief and our behavior. Our belief determines where we spend eternity. Our behavior determines how we spend eternity.

Why will God judge the works of believers?

_____

_____

_____

_____

Key Verses

1 Corinthians 3:5–15; Matthew 6:1–4; 11:21–24; Revelation 20:11–13

What truths stand out to you as you read these verses?

_____

_____

What is the Holy Spirit saying to you through these Scriptures?

_____

_____

Key Question

Matthew 6:4 says that the Father *"will Himself reward you openly"* for your works. How does this affect your desire to please God through your behavior on earth?

Key Prayer

Father, thank You for making a way for us to go to heaven through Jesus. Thank You that when we believe in You, You work within us to give us the desire to obey You. Help us choose good works on earth that are of eternal significance. In Jesus' name, Amen.

5

A GLORIOUS DAY

Jesus is coming again, but until He does, our job is to love and serve people and share the gospel.

RECAP
In the previous session, we learned that everyone will be judged for their works. Believers will be rewarded for their works at the judgment seat of Christ, and unbelievers will be punished for their works at the Great White Throne judgment. Which judgment we attend depends on whether we believe in Jesus.

How did understanding that your behavior and works matter affect the decisions you made this past week?

ENGAGE
What is your dream vacation?

WATCH
Watch "A Glorious Day."
- Look for what Jesus says to do while we wait on earth for His return.
- Watch for the pitfalls in how we look at end times prophecy.

(If you are not able to watch this teaching on video, read the following. Otherwise, skip to the **Talk** section after viewing.)

READ

I t is easy to get consumed with prophetic charts and Second Coming teachings or to sit back and just wait complacently for Jesus to appear. I believe both of those responses are inspired by the enemy who wants us not to do what Jesus commanded.

Do Business Till I Come

This passage from Luke shows Jesus' teaching about what we should do while waiting for His return. It shows, as we saw last week, that both believers and unbelievers will be judged. It also shows that we have a job to do:

> Now as they heard these things, He spoke another parable, because He was near Jerusalem and because they thought the kingdom of God would appear immediately. Therefore He said: "A certain nobleman went into a far country to receive for himself a kingdom and to return. So he called ten of his servants, delivered to them ten minas, and said to them, 'Do business till I come.' But his citizens hated him, and sent a delegation after him, saying, 'We will not have this *man* to reign over us.'
>
> "And so it was that when he returned, having received the kingdom, he then commanded these servants, to whom he had given the money, to be called to him, that he might know how much every man had gained by trading. Then came the first, saying, 'Master, your mina has earned ten minas.' And he said to him, 'Well *done,* good servant; because you were faithful in a very little, have

authority over ten cities.' And the second came, saying, 'Master, your mina has earned five minas.' Likewise he said to him, 'You also be over five cities.'

"Then another came, saying, 'Master, here is your mina, which I have kept put away in a handkerchief. For I feared you, because you are an austere man. You collect what you did not deposit, and reap what you did not sow.' And he said to him, 'Out of your own mouth I will judge you, *you* wicked servant. You knew that I was an austere man, collecting what I did not deposit and reaping what I did not sow. Why then did you not put my money in the bank, that at my coming I might have collected it with interest?'

"And he said to those who stood by, 'Take the mina from him, and give *it* to him who has ten minas.' (But they said to him, 'Master, he has ten minas.') 'For I say to you, that to everyone who has will be given; and from him who does not have, even what he has will be taken away from him. But bring here those enemies of mine, who did not want me to reign over them, and slay *them* before me'" (Luke 19:11–27).

The servants who were given minas were believers. The citizens were unbelievers. The servants were to "do business until He comes." Some of the modern end times teachings pull us away from our focus on our job here and now. We are to focus on sharing the gospel throughout the world. Every time we give, every time we love, every time we serve, every time we witness or share the gospel, we are doing business until He comes.

Don't Get Sidetracked

In Matthew 24, Jesus talks very directly about His coming and the end of the age:

> Now as He sat on the Mount of Olives, the disciples came to Him privately, saying, "Tell us, when will these things be? And what *will be* the sign of Your coming, and of the end of the age?"
>
> And Jesus answered and said to them: "Take heed that no one deceives you. For many will come in My name, saying, 'I am the Christ,' and will deceive many. And you will hear of wars and rumors of wars. See that you are not troubled; for all *these things* must come to pass, but the end is not yet. For nation will rise against nation, and kingdom against kingdom. And there will be famines, pestilences, and earthquakes in various places. All these *are* the beginning of sorrows.
>
> Then they will deliver you up to tribulation and kill you, and you will be hated by all nations for My name's sake. And then many will be offended, will betray one another, and will hate one another. Then many false prophets will rise up and deceive many. And because lawlessness will abound, the love of many will grow cold. But he who endures to the end shall be saved. And this gospel of the kingdom will be preached in all the world as a witness to all the nations, and then the end will come" (Matthew 24:3-14).

Jesus says many will be deceived—or sidetracked—by people, prophecies, and events. Virtually every generation has had these signs. But the key idea is that the gospel will be preached to all the nations, and *then* the end will come. So we still have a job to do.

Modern day teaching about the second coming has sidetracked us. There has been argument about this for centuries. We argued about it in Bible school: "What kind of rapture do you believe in?" This is the same argument my teacher in Bible school said they had when he was in school.

Then there is speculation about the Antichrist. Every generation for the last 150 years has identified the Antichrist; Mussolini, Hitler, Henry Kissinger, Prince Charles, and even some presidents have been identified as the Antichrist. It can be fun to dabble in the speculative word of prophecy, but then we become opinionated and divisive. There have also been so many dates set for the second coming, even in my lifetime. But Jesus says, "But of that day and hour no one knows, not even the angels of heaven, but My Father only" (Matthew 24:36).

The modern teaching about the rapture and tribulation is relatively new; it has only been around for about 150 years. It is also espoused only by English-speaking people because it has only been included in the footnotes of English Bibles.

Another neatly packaged theory was that when Greece joined the common market, that made 10 nations, and the Roman Empire was restored. Except that Ireland is part of the common market, which was not part of the Roman Empire. And now there are 27 nations in the common market.

My and Gateway's view on this is simple: Jesus is coming.

Twenty-One Irrefutable Facts of the Second Coming.
1. Jesus Himself will come again. (1 Thessalonians 4:16)
2. Jesus Himself will receive us. (John 14:3)
3. We will meet Him in the air. (1 Thessalonians 4:17)
4. He will minister to those who are found watchful. (Luke 12:37)
5. He will return to earth. (Acts 1:11)
6. He will return to the Mount of Olives. (Zechariah 14:4)
7. He will return in flaming fire. (2 Thessalonians 1:7-8)
8. He will come with power and great glory. (Matthew 24:30)
9. He will stand on earth. (Job 19:25)
10. He will destroy the Antichrist. (2 Thessalonians 2:8)
11. He will sit on the throne of His glory. (Matthew 25:31)
12. He will be given the throne of David. (Luke 1:32)
13. He will be given the nations. (Psalm 2:8)
14. He will gather all nations and judge them. (Matthew 25:32)
15. He will reign on the earth. (Jeremiah 23:5)
16. He will be given the kingdoms of this world. (Revelation 11:15)
17. He will be given dominion. (Daniel 7:14)
18. All who are in the graves will hear His voice. (John 5:28)
19. Every eye will see Him. (Revelation 1:7)
20. Every knee will bow. (Isaiah 45:22-23 and Philippians 2:9-11)
21. We can hasten the coming of the Lord. (2 Peter 3:12)

The word for hastening is *speudo*, which means "to cause something to happen soon, to hurry something up." We get our English word *speed* from this word.

We can make a difference. Do business until He comes. Don't be sidetracked. The one truth and sign that we need to focus on is that this gospel must be preached in the whole world.

NOTES

_____

_____

_____

_____

_____

_____

_____

_____

_____

_____

_____

_____

TALK

These questions can be used for group discussion or personal reflection:

Question 1

When did you first hear about the Second Coming of Christ? What did you imagine it would be like?

_____

_____

_____

_____

Question 2

Read 1 Thessalonians 4:16–18, Matthew 24:30, and Philippians 2:9–11. What are you most looking forward to about Christ's return?

_____

_____

_____

_____

Question 3

Are you more likely to wrestle with complacency toward Christ's return or over-analysis of the end times? How does each approach work against the body of Christ?

_____

_____

_____

_____

Question 4

Second Peter 3:12 says that we can hasten the coming of the day of God. How can we do that, according to Matthew 24:14?

_____

_____

_____

_____

PRAY

If studying alone, ask the Holy Spirit to reveal the truth about Himself to you. If in a group, take some time to pray for each other as you think about the truths discussed in this session.

EXPLORE

Do you want to go deeper with this teaching? Here are some additional things to think about, pray for, or write about in your journal throughout the next week:

Key Quote

> *Every time we give, every time we love, every time we serve, every time we witness or share the gospel, we are doing business until He comes.*

To do business until Christ comes means to do more than just believe. He wants us to give, love, serve, and share the gospel with others. What do you believe the Lord is specifically asking you to do to "hasten" His return?

_____

_____

_____

_____

Key Verses

Luke 19:11–27; Matthew 24:3–14, 36

What truths stand out to you as you read these verses?

_____

_____

What is the Holy Spirit saying to you through these Scriptures?

_____

_____

Key Question
What do you need to do to prepare for Christ's return?

Key Prayer
Heavenly Father, thank You that Jesus will one day return in glory and power. Thank You for making a way for everybody to be saved. Help us to share the gospel with friends and loved ones who do not yet know You. May we continue to do business until Jesus returns. In Jesus' name, Amen.

LEADER'S GUIDE

The End... What Happens Next? Leader's Guide is designed to help you lead your small group or class through *The End... What Happens Next?* curriculum. Use this guide along with the curriculum for a life-changing, interactive experience.

BEFORE YOU MEET

- Ask God to prepare the hearts and minds of the people in your group. Ask Him to show you how to encourage each person to integrate the principles all of you discover into your daily lives through group discussion and writing in your journals.
- Preview the video segment for the week.
- Plan how much time you'll give to each portion of your meeting (see the suggested schedule below). In case you're unable to get through all of the activities in the time you have planned, here is a list of the most important questions (from the **Talk** section) for each week.

SUGGESTED SCHEDULE FOR THE GROUP:

1. **Engage** and **Recap** (5 Minutes)
2. **Watch** or **Read** (20 Minutes)
3. **Talk** (25 Minutes)
4. **Pray** (10 minutes)

SESSION ONE

Q: What do you think people are really wrestling with when they ask, "How could a loving God send anyone to hell?

Q: Why is rejecting God "inexcusable" and "rebellious"?

SESSION TWO

Q: Why do you think it's so hard to imagine what heaven will be like?

Q: Have you ever worried that heaven will be boring? Why do you think many people believe that way?

SESSION THREE

Q: Read Luke 16:19–31. What do you think Jesus wanted to communicate to us through this story?

Q: What are the physical and emotional properties on earth that keep us mentally stable? How will hell be different from earth?

SESSION FOUR

Q: What is the main difference between the judgment seat of Christ and the Great White Throne judgment?

Q: According to Matthew 6:1–4, how can believers lose their reward for good works?

SESSION FIVE

Q: Are you more likely to wrestle with complacency toward Christ's return or over-analysis of the end times? How does each approach work against the body of Christ?

Q: Second Peter 3:12 says that we can hasten the coming of the day of God. How can we do that, according to Matthew 24:14?

Remember, the goal is not necessarily to get through all of the questions. The highest priority is for the group to learn and engage in a dynamic discussion.

HOW TO USE THE CURRICULUM:

This study has a simple design.

EACH WEEK:

The One Thing:
This is a brief statement under each session title that sums up the main point—the key idea—of the session.

Recap:
Recap the previous week's session, inviting members to share about any opportunities they have encountered throughout the week that apply what they learned (this doesn't apply to the first week).

Engage:
Ask the icebreaker question to help get people talking and feeling comfortable with one another.

Watch:
Watch the videos (recommended).

Read:
If you're unable to watch the videos, read these sections.

Talk:
The questions in these lessons are intentionally open-ended. Use them to help the group members reflect on Scripture and the lesson.

Pray:
Ask members to share their concerns and then pray together. Be sensitive to the Holy Spirit and the needs of the group.

Explore:
Encourage members to complete the written portion in their books before the next meeting.

KEY TIPS FOR THE LEADER:

- Generate participation and discussion.
- Resist the urge to teach. The goal is for great conversation that leads to discovery.
- Ask open-ended questions—questions that can't be answered with "yes" or "no" (e.g., "What do you think about that?" rather than "Do you agree?")
- When a question arises, ask the group for their input instead of answering it yourself before allowing anyone else to respond.
- Be comfortable with silence. If you ask a question and no one responds, rephrase the question and wait for a response. Your primary role is to create an environment where people feel comfortable to be themselves and participate, not to provide the answers to all of their questions.
- Ask the group to pray for each other from week to week, especially about key issues that arise during your group time. This is how you begin to build authentic community and encourage spiritual growth within the group.

KEYS TO A DYNAMIC SMALL GROUP:

Relationships

Meaningful, encouraging relationships are the foundation of a dynamic small group. Teaching, discussion, worship, and prayer

are important elements of a group meeting, but the depth of each
element is often dependent upon the depth of the relationships
between members.

Availability

Building a sense of community within your group requires members
to prioritize their relationships with one another. This means being
available to listen, care for one another, and meet each other's
needs.

Mutual Respect

Mutual respect is shown when members value each other's
opinions (even when they disagree) and are careful never to put
down or embarrass others in the group (including their spouses,
who may or may not be present).

Openness

A healthy small group environment encourages sincerity and
transparency. Members treat each other with grace in areas of
weakness, allowing each other room to grow.

Confidentiality

To develop authenticity and a sense of safety within the group,
each member must be able to trust that things discussed within the
group will not be shared outside the group.

Shared Responsibility

Group members will share the responsibility of group meetings by using their God-given abilities to serve at each gathering. Some may greet, some may host, some may teach, etc. Ideally, each person should be available to care for others as needed.

Sensitivity

Dynamic small groups are born when the leader consistently seeks and is responsive to the guidance of the Holy Spirit, following His leading throughout the meeting as opposed to sticking to the "agenda." This guidance is especially important during the discussion and ministry time.

Fun!

Dynamic small groups take the time to have fun! Create an atmosphere for fun, and be willing to laugh at yourself every now and then!

ABOUT THE AUTHOR

Robert Morris is the lead senior pastor of Gateway Church, a multicampus church in the Dallas/Fort Worth Metroplex. Since it began in 2000, the church has grown to more than 39,000 active members. His television program is aired in over 190 countries, and his radio feature, *Worship & the Word with Pastor Robert*, airs on radio stations across America. He serves as chancellor of The King's University and is the bestselling author of 15 books including *The Blessed Life, Truly Free, Frequency*, and *Beyond Blessed*. Robert and his wife, Debbie, have been married 38 years and are blessed with one married daughter, two married sons, and nine grandchildren. He lives in Dallas, TX.

More resources for your small group by Pastor Robert Morris!

Study Guide: 978-1-945529-54-2
DVD: 978-1-949399-41-7

Study Guide: 978-1-949399-54-7
DVD: 978-1-949399-51-6

Study Guide: 978-1-945529-51-1
DVD: 978-1-949399-49-3

Study Guide: 978-1-945529-71-9
DVD: 978-1-949399-50-9

DVD + Discussion Guide:
978-1-949399-68-4

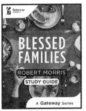

Study Guide: 978-1-949399-55-4
DVD: 978-1-949399-52-3

Study Guide: 978-1-945529-85-6
DVD: 978-1-949399-48-6

Study Guide: 978-1-945529-56-6
DVD: 978-1-949399-43-1

Study Guide: 978-1-945529-55-9
DVD: 978-1-949399-42-4

Study Guide: 978-1-945529-88-7
DVD: 978-1-949399-53-0

Study Guide: 978-1-949399-65-3
DVD: 978-1-949399-66-0

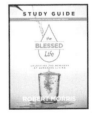

Study Guide: 978-0-997429-84-8
DVD: 978-1-949399-46-2

You can find these resources and others at
www.gatewaypublishing.com